Phonics Games — LEVEL B

Correlated
to State Standards

Visit
www.teaching-standards.com
to view a correlation of
this book's activities
to your state's standards.
This is a free service.

EMC 3363

Evan-Moor®
EDUCATIONAL PUBLISHERS
Helping Children Learn since 1979

Editorial   Joy Evans
Development: Camille Liscinsky
           Jo Ellen Moore
           Lisa Vitarisi Mathews
Copy Editing: Carrie Gwynne
           Laurie Westrich
Cover/Illustrations: Liliana Potigian/Jo Larsen
Art Direction: Cheryl Puckett
Design/Production: Marcia Smith
           Olivia C. Trinidad

Congratulations on your purchase of some of the finest teaching materials in the world.

Photocopying the pages in this book is permitted for <u>single-classroom use only</u>*. Making photocopies for additional classes or schools is prohibited.*

How to Use
Phonics Games

LEVEL B

Play the games as a follow-up to a phonics lesson, or use a game to target a skill that several students need to practice. The games are also fun "extra-time" or rainy-day recess activities.

Model how to play each type of game, and place the games in an area of your classroom that is easily accessible to students.

Games Include:

Directions

Game boards

Game cards

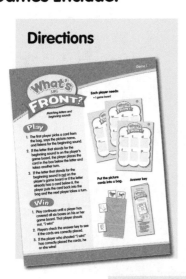

Answer key

Reproducible activity pages

How to Make a Phonics Game

Steps to Follow:

1. Laminate the directions page, the game boards, the cards, and the answer key(s).

2. Reproduce the activity pages.

3. Place the laminated game supplies and any additional items, such as bean markers or brown paper bags, in a folder that has a closure.

Materials

- laminator
- scissors
- brown paper bags
- game board markers such as beans
- folder that has a closure

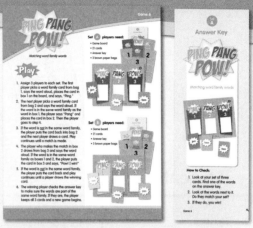

Directions page   Answer key

Game boards

Game cards

Reproducible activity pages

Phonics Games Checklist

LEVEL B

Student	Games Played	What's Up Front? Beginning Sounds	Concentration Ending Sounds	Go Pick! Rhyming Words	Concentration Short Vowel Sounds	4-in-a-row CVC Words	Ping Pang Pow! Word Family Words	Spell It! CVC Words

EMC 3363 • © Evan-Moor Corp.

What's UP FRONT?

Matching letters and beginning sounds

Play

1. The first player picks a card from the bag, says the picture name, and listens for the beginning sound.

2. If the letter that stands for the beginning sound is on the player's game board, the player places the card in the box below the letter and takes another turn.

3. If the letter that stands for the beginning sound is <u>not</u> on the player's game board or if the letter already has a card below it, the player puts the card back into the bag and the next player takes a turn.

Win

1. Play continues until a player has covered all six boxes on his or her game board. That player shouts out, "I win!"

2. Players check the answer key to see if the cards are correctly placed.

3. If the player who shouted "I win!" has correctly placed the cards, he or she wins!

Each player needs:

• 1 game board

Put the picture cards into a bag.

Answer key

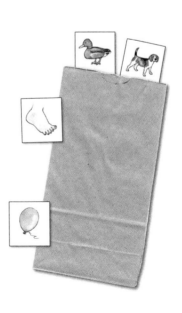

Phonics Games, Level B • EMC 3363 • © Evan-Moor Corp.

What's UP FRONT?

1

h____ f____ b____

r____ s____ p____

Game 1

Phonics Games, Level B
EMC 3363 • © Evan-Moor Corp.

What's UP FRONT?

m_____   l_____   t_____

n_____   b_____   p_____

Game 1

Phonics Games, Level B
EMC 3363 • © Evan-Moor Corp.

What's UP FRONT?

w____   d____   r____

s____   h____   l____

Game 1

Phonics Games, Level B
EMC 3363 • © Evan-Moor Corp.

What's UP FRONT?

w____   t____   d____

f____   l____   p____

Game 1

Phonics Games, Level B
EMC 3363 • © Evan-Moor Corp.

What's UP FRONT?

n_____

w_____

r_____

d_____

m_____

h_____

Game 1

Phonics Games, Level B
EMC 3363 • © Evan-Moor Corp.

What's UP FRONT?

b____   s____   n____

m____   f____   t____

Game 1

Phonics Games, Level B
EMC 3363 • © Evan-Moor Corp.

Game 1

Phonics Games, Level B
EMC 3363
© Evan-Moor Corp.

Game 1

Phonics Games, Level B
EMC 3363
© Evan-Moor Corp.

Game 1

Phonics Games, Level B
EMC 3363
© Evan-Moor Corp.

Game 1

Phonics Games, Level B
EMC 3363
© Evan-Moor Corp.

Game 1

Phonics Games, Level B
EMC 3363
© Evan-Moor Corp.

Game 1

Phonics Games, Level B
EMC 3363
© Evan-Moor Corp.

Game 1

Phonics Games, Level B
EMC 3363
© Evan-Moor Corp.

Game 1

Phonics Games, Level B
EMC 3363
© Evan-Moor Corp.

Game 1

Phonics Games, Level B
EMC 3363
© Evan-Moor Corp.

Game 1

Phonics Games, Level B
EMC 3363
© Evan-Moor Corp.

Game 1

Phonics Games, Level B
EMC 3363
© Evan-Moor Corp.

Game 1

Phonics Games, Level B
EMC 3363
© Evan-Moor Corp.

Game 1

Phonics Games, Level B
EMC 3363
© Evan-Moor Corp.

Game 1

Phonics Games, Level B
EMC 3363
© Evan-Moor Corp.

Game 1

Phonics Games, Level B
EMC 3363
© Evan-Moor Corp.

Game 1

Phonics Games, Level B
EMC 3363
© Evan-Moor Corp.

Game 1

Phonics Games, Level B
EMC 3363
© Evan-Moor Corp.

Game 1

Phonics Games, Level B
EMC 3363
© Evan-Moor Corp.

Game 1

Phonics Games, Level B
EMC 3363
© Evan-Moor Corp.

Game 1

Phonics Games, Level B
EMC 3363
© Evan-Moor Corp.

Game 1

Phonics Games, Level B
EMC 3363
© Evan-Moor Corp.

Game 1

Phonics Games, Level B
EMC 3363
© Evan-Moor Corp.

Game 1

Phonics Games, Level B
EMC 3363
© Evan-Moor Corp.

Game 1

Phonics Games, Level B
EMC 3363
© Evan-Moor Corp.

Game 1

Phonics Games, Level B
EMC 3363
© Evan-Moor Corp.

Game 1

Phonics Games, Level B
EMC 3363
© Evan-Moor Corp.

Game 1

Phonics Games, Level B
EMC 3363
© Evan-Moor Corp.

Game 1

Phonics Games, Level B
EMC 3363
© Evan-Moor Corp.

Game 1

Phonics Games, Level B
EMC 3363
© Evan-Moor Corp.

Game 1

Phonics Games, Level B
EMC 3363
© Evan-Moor Corp.

Game 1

Phonics Games, Level B
EMC 3363
© Evan-Moor Corp.

Game 1

Phonics Games, Level B
EMC 3363
© Evan-Moor Corp.

Game 1

Phonics Games, Level B
EMC 3363
© Evan-Moor Corp.

Game 1

Phonics Games, Level B
EMC 3363
© Evan-Moor Corp.

Game 1

Phonics Games, Level B
EMC 3363
© Evan-Moor Corp.

Game 1

Phonics Games, Level B
EMC 3363
© Evan-Moor Corp.

Game 1

Phonics Games, Level B
EMC 3363
© Evan-Moor Corp.

Game 1

Phonics Games, Level B
EMC 3363
© Evan-Moor Corp.

Game 1

Phonics Games, Level B
EMC 3363
© Evan-Moor Corp.

Game 1

Phonics Games, Level B
EMC 3363
© Evan-Moor Corp.

What's UP FRONT?

Matching letters and beginning sounds

How to Check:

1. Look at the first letter on your game board. Find the letter on the answer key.

2. Check to see if one of the pictures below the letter is the picture you placed on your game board.

3. Check each of the letters on your game board.

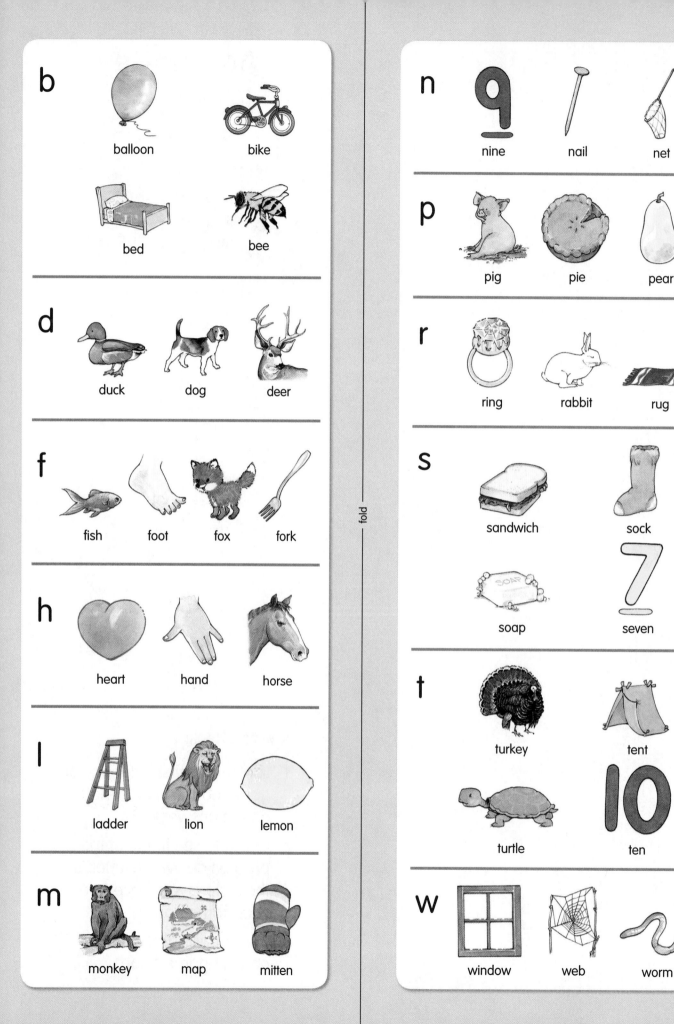

b
balloon
bike
bed
bee

d
duck
dog
deer

f
fish
foot
fox
fork

h
heart
hand
horse

l
ladder
lion
lemon

m
monkey
map
mitten

n
nine
nail
net

p
pig
pie
pear

r
ring
rabbit
rug

s
sandwich
sock
soap
seven

t
turkey
tent
turtle
ten

w
window
web
worm

fold

Animal Sounds

Say each animal name. Listen for the beginning sound.
Circle the letter that stands for the beginning sound you hear.

1.

b t m

2.

p r t

3.

p s b

4.

d r l

5.

g l m

6.

m w h

7.

d s p

8.

t h k

9.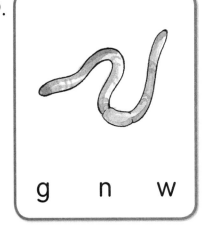

g n w

What's the Sound?

Say each picture name. Listen for the beginning sound.
Cut out and glue the letter that stands for the beginning sound.

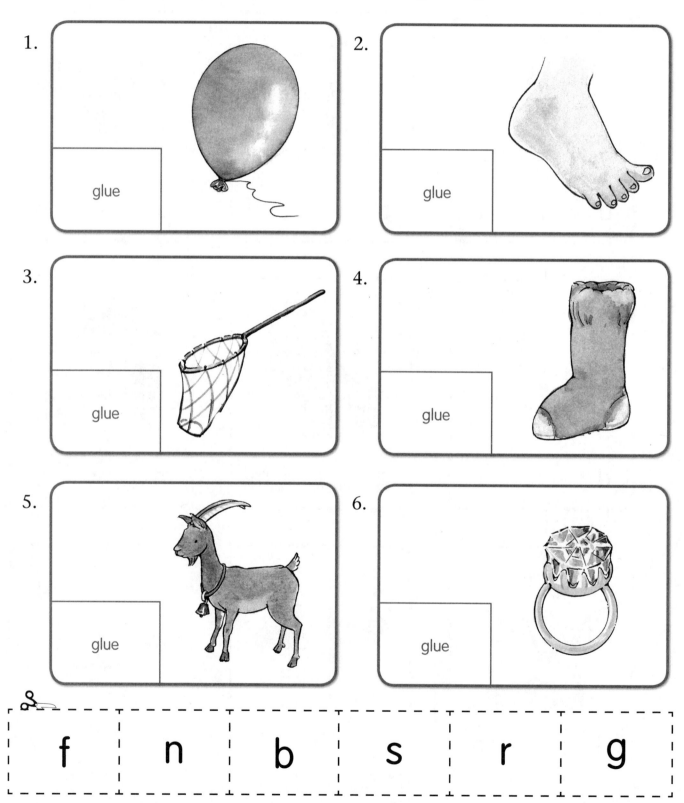

1.
glue

2.
glue

3.
glue

4.
glue

5.
glue

6.
glue

f n b s r g

  Phonics Games, Level B • EMC 3363 • © Evan-Moor Corp.

Concentration

Matching ending sounds

Play

1. Place each set of cards facedown in six rows of four. Assign three players to each set.

2. The first player turns over one picture card and one letter card and says the picture name aloud.

3. If the letter on the card stands for the ending sound of the picture name, the player keeps the cards and takes another turn.

4. If the letter on the card does <u>not</u> stand for the ending sound of the picture name, the player turns the cards over and the next player takes a turn.

Win

1. The game continues until all of the cards are matched.

2. Players look at the answer key to see if their pairs are correctly matched.

3. The player with the most pairs wins!

Set A players need:

- 24 purple cards
- Answer key

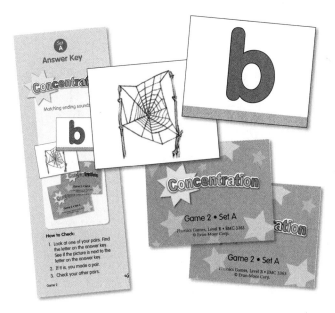

Set B players need:

- 24 orange cards
- Answer key

Phonics Games, Level B • EMC 3363 • © Evan-Moor Corp.

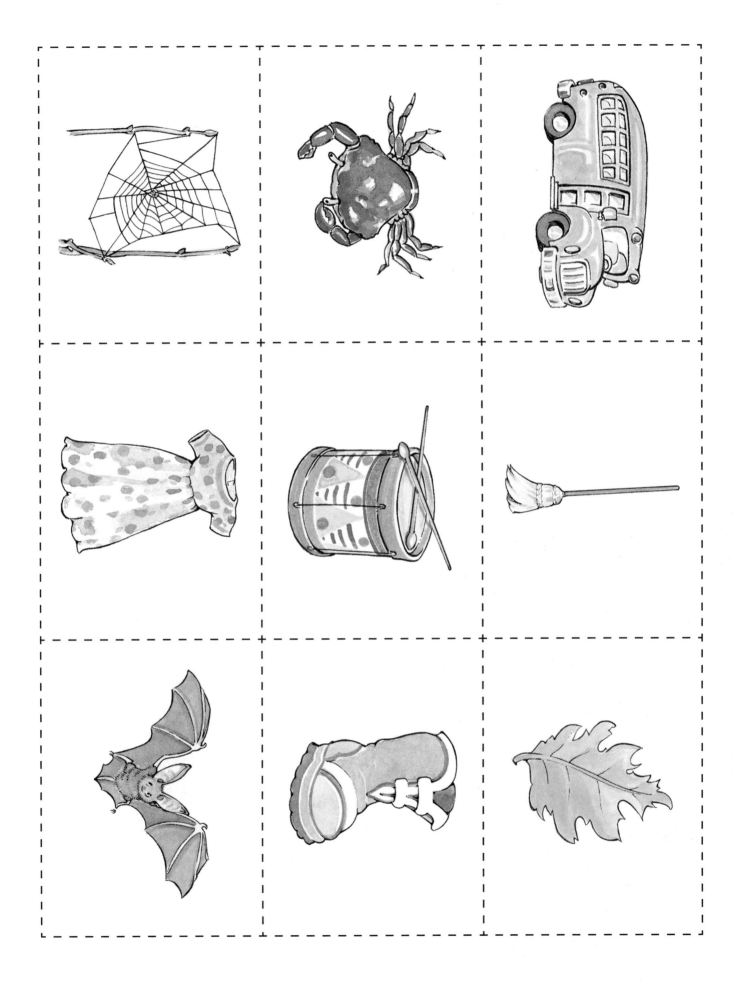

Concentration

Game 2 • Set A

Phonics Games, Level B • EMC 3363
© Evan-Moor Corp.

Concentration

Game 2 • Set A

Phonics Games, Level B • EMC 3363
© Evan-Moor Corp.

Concentration

Game 2 • Set A

Phonics Games, Level B • EMC 3363
© Evan-Moor Corp.

Concentration

Game 2 • Set A

Phonics Games, Level B • EMC 3363
© Evan-Moor Corp.

Concentration

Game 2 • Set A

Phonics Games, Level B • EMC 3363
© Evan-Moor Corp.

Concentration

Game 2 • Set A

Phonics Games, Level B • EMC 3363
© Evan-Moor Corp.

Concentration

Game 2 • Set A

Phonics Games, Level B • EMC 3363
© Evan-Moor Corp.

Concentration

Game 2 • Set A

Phonics Games, Level B • EMC 3363
© Evan-Moor Corp.

Concentration

Game 2 • Set A

Phonics Games, Level B • EMC 3363
© Evan-Moor Corp.

Concentration

Game 2 • Set A

Phonics Games, Level B • EMC 3363
© Evan-Moor Corp.

Concentration

Game 2 • Set A

Phonics Games, Level B • EMC 3363
© Evan-Moor Corp.

Concentration

Game 2 • Set A

Phonics Games, Level B • EMC 3363
© Evan-Moor Corp.

Concentration

Game 2 • Set A

Phonics Games, Level B • EMC 3363
© Evan-Moor Corp.

Concentration

Game 2 • Set A

Phonics Games, Level B • EMC 3363
© Evan-Moor Corp.

Concentration

Game 2 • Set A

Phonics Games, Level B • EMC 3363
© Evan-Moor Corp.

Concentration

Game 2 • Set A

Phonics Games, Level B • EMC 3363
© Evan-Moor Corp.

Concentration

Game 2 • Set A

Phonics Games, Level B • EMC 3363
© Evan-Moor Corp.

Concentration

Game 2 • Set A

Phonics Games, Level B • EMC 3363
© Evan-Moor Corp.

Concentration

Game 2 • Set A

Phonics Games, Level B • EMC 3363
© Evan-Moor Corp.

Concentration

Game 2 • Set A

Phonics Games, Level B • EMC 3363
© Evan-Moor Corp.

Concentration

Game 2 • Set A

Phonics Games, Level B • EMC 3363
© Evan-Moor Corp.

Concentration

Game 2 • Set A

Phonics Games, Level B • EMC 3363
© Evan-Moor Corp.

Concentration

Game 2 • Set A

Phonics Games, Level B • EMC 3363
© Evan-Moor Corp.

Concentration

Game 2 • Set A

Phonics Games, Level B • EMC 3363
© Evan-Moor Corp.

Concentration

Game 2 • Set B

Phonics Games, Level B • EMC 3363
© Evan-Moor Corp.

Concentration

Game 2 • Set B

Phonics Games, Level B • EMC 3363
© Evan-Moor Corp.

Concentration

Game 2 • Set B

Phonics Games, Level B • EMC 3363
© Evan-Moor Corp.

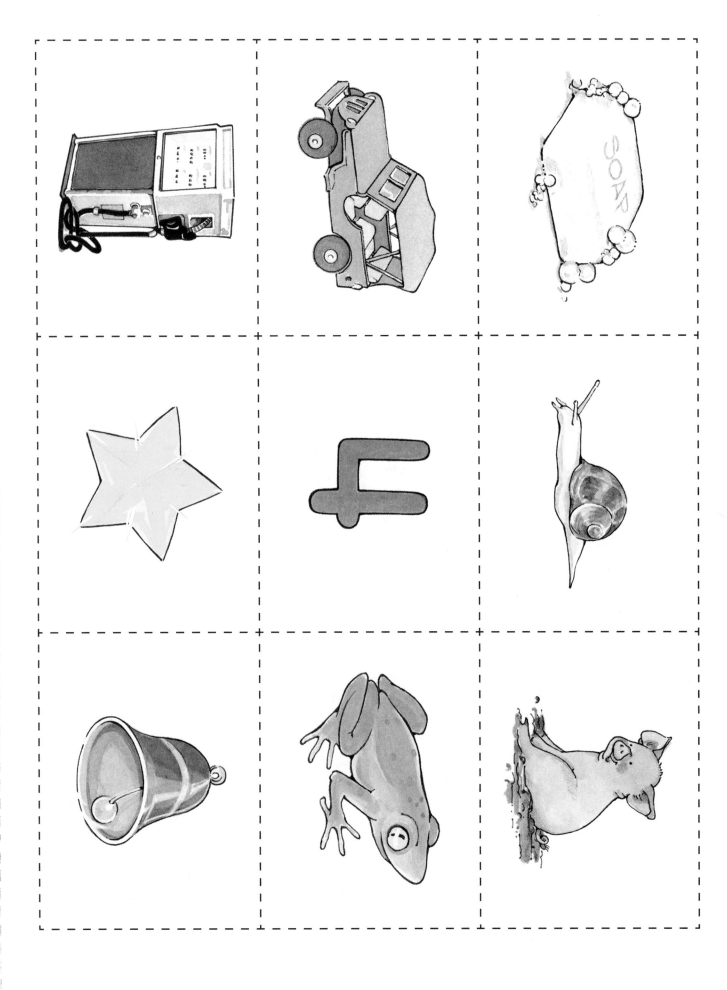

Concentration

Game 2 • Set B

Phonics Games, Level B • EMC 3363
© Evan-Moor Corp.

Concentration

Game 2 • Set B

Phonics Games, Level B • EMC 3363
© Evan-Moor Corp.

Concentration

Game 2 • Set B

Phonics Games, Level B • EMC 3363
© Evan-Moor Corp.

Concentration

Game 2 • Set B

Phonics Games, Level B • EMC 3363
© Evan-Moor Corp.

Concentration

Game 2 • Set B

Phonics Games, Level B • EMC 3363
© Evan-Moor Corp.

Concentration

Game 2 • Set B

Phonics Games, Level B • EMC 3363
© Evan-Moor Corp.

Concentration

Game 2 • Set B

Phonics Games, Level B • EMC 3363
© Evan-Moor Corp.

Concentration

Game 2 • Set B

Phonics Games, Level B • EMC 3363
© Evan-Moor Corp.

Concentration

Game 2 • Set B

Phonics Games, Level B • EMC 3363
© Evan-Moor Corp.

n   n   s

s   p   p

r   r   l

Concentration

Game 2 • Set B

Phonics Games, Level B • EMC 3363
© Evan-Moor Corp.

Concentration

Game 2 • Set B

Phonics Games, Level B • EMC 3363
© Evan-Moor Corp.

Concentration

Game 2 • Set B

Phonics Games, Level B • EMC 3363
© Evan-Moor Corp.

Concentration

Game 2 • Set B

Phonics Games, Level B • EMC 3363
© Evan-Moor Corp.

Concentration

Game 2 • Set B

Phonics Games, Level B • EMC 3363
© Evan-Moor Corp.

Concentration

Game 2 • Set B

Phonics Games, Level B • EMC 3363
© Evan-Moor Corp.

Concentration

Game 2 • Set B

Phonics Games, Level B • EMC 3363
© Evan-Moor Corp.

Concentration

Game 2 • Set B

Phonics Games, Level B • EMC 3363
© Evan-Moor Corp.

Concentration

Game 2 • Set B

Phonics Games, Level B • EMC 3363
© Evan-Moor Corp.

Concentration

Game 2 • Set B

Phonics Games, Level B • EMC 3363
© Evan-Moor Corp.

Concentration

Game 2 • Set B

Phonics Games, Level B • EMC 3363
© Evan-Moor Corp.

Concentration

Game 2 • Set B

Phonics Games, Level B • EMC 3363
© Evan-Moor Corp.

Answer Key

Matching ending sounds

Game 2 • Set A
Phonics Games, Level B • EMC 3363
© Evan-Moor Corp.

Game 2 • Set A
Phonics Games, Level B • EMC 3363
© Evan-Moor Corp.

How to Check:

1. Look at one of your pairs. Find the letter on the answer key. See if the picture is next to the letter on the answer key.

2. If it is, you made a pair.

3. Check your other pairs.

Game 2

Answer Key

Matching ending sounds

Game 2 • Set B
Phonics Games, Level B • EMC 3363
© Evan-Moor Corp.

Game 2 • Set B
Phonics Games, Level B • EMC 3363
© Evan-Moor Corp.

How to Check:

1. Look at one of your pairs. Find the letter on the answer key. See if the picture is next to the letter on the answer key.

2. If it is, you made a pair.

3. Check your other pairs.

Game 2

n		
	wagon	sun
s		
	grass	gas
p		
	jeep	soap
r		
	star	four
l		
	snail	bell
g		
	frog	pig

b	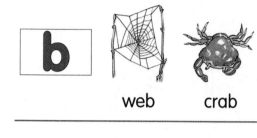	
	web	crab
s	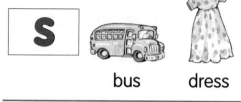	
	bus	dress
m		
	drum	broom
t	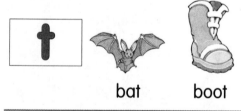	
	bat	boot
f		
	leaf	roof
k	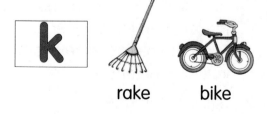	
	rake	bike

Name _____

How Does It End?

Say each animal name. Listen for the ending sound.
Circle the letter that stands for the ending sound you hear.

1.

   t   c   f

2.

   b   l   g

3.

   r   d   s

4.

   m   s   g

5.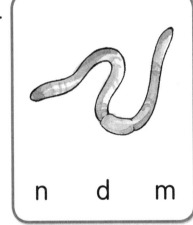

   n   d   m

6.

   l   w   k

7.

   r   t   p

8.

   b   l   f

9.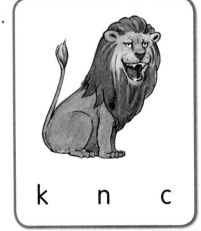

   k   n   c

End It

Say each picture name. Listen for the ending sound.
Draw a line from each picture to its ending sound.

1.  •

2.  •

3.  •

4.  •

5.   •

6.  •

7.  •

8.   •

• k

• t

• p

• f

• n

• m

• l

• s

Go Pick!

Matching rhyming words

Play

1. Players sit in a circle holding their cards from each other's view. The remaining cards are placed facedown in a pile in the middle of the circle.

2. Players looks at their cards and lay any rhyming pairs they have faceup.

3. Then the first player asks the player to the left for a rhyming card. For example: *Do you have a rhyme for **log**?*

4. If the player to the left has a rhyming word, he or she gives the card to the first player, who sets the pair down and takes another turn.

5. If the player to the left does <u>not</u> have a rhyming word, he or she tells the first player "Go pick!" The player picks a card from the pile and if the word rhymes, the player makes a pair and sets it down. If the word does <u>not</u> rhyme, the player adds the card to his or her hand.

Win

1. Play continues counterclockwise until all of the cards have been matched.

2. Each player looks at the answer key to check that cards are correctly matched.

3. The player with the most pairs wins!

Give each player 5 game cards.

Answer key

Phonics Games, Level B • EMC 3363 • © Evan-Moor Corp.

cat

hat

bag

wag

top

mop

bug

rug

dog

log

sock

rock

Game 3

Phonics Games, Level B
EMC 3363
© Evan-Moor Corp.

Game 3

Phonics Games, Level B
EMC 3363
© Evan-Moor Corp.

Game 3

Phonics Games, Level B
EMC 3363
© Evan-Moor Corp.

Game 3

Phonics Games, Level B
EMC 3363
© Evan-Moor Corp.

Game 3

Phonics Games, Level B
EMC 3363
© Evan-Moor Corp.

Game 3

Phonics Games, Level B
EMC 3363
© Evan-Moor Corp.

Game 3

Phonics Games, Level B
EMC 3363
© Evan-Moor Corp.

Game 3

Phonics Games, Level B
EMC 3363
© Evan-Moor Corp.

Game 3

Phonics Games, Level B
EMC 3363
© Evan-Moor Corp.

Game 3

Phonics Games, Level B
EMC 3363
© Evan-Moor Corp.

Game 3

Phonics Games, Level B
EMC 3363
© Evan-Moor Corp.

Game 3

Phonics Games, Level B
EMC 3363
© Evan-Moor Corp.

star	car	pen	ten
bed	red	bee	three
net	jet	can	fan

Game 3

Phonics Games, Level B
EMC 3363
© Evan-Moor Corp.

Game 3

Phonics Games, Level B
EMC 3363
© Evan-Moor Corp.

Game 3

Phonics Games, Level B
EMC 3363
© Evan-Moor Corp.

Game 3

Phonics Games, Level B
EMC 3363
© Evan-Moor Corp.

Game 3

Phonics Games, Level B
EMC 3363
© Evan-Moor Corp.

Game 3

Phonics Games, Level B
EMC 3363
© Evan-Moor Corp.

Game 3

Phonics Games, Level B
EMC 3363
© Evan-Moor Corp.

Game 3

Phonics Games, Level B
EMC 3363
© Evan-Moor Corp.

Game 3

Phonics Games, Level B
EMC 3363
© Evan-Moor Corp.

Game 3

Phonics Games, Level B
EMC 3363
© Evan-Moor Corp.

Game 3

Phonics Games, Level B
EMC 3363
© Evan-Moor Corp.

Game 3

Phonics Games, Level B
EMC 3363
© Evan-Moor Corp.

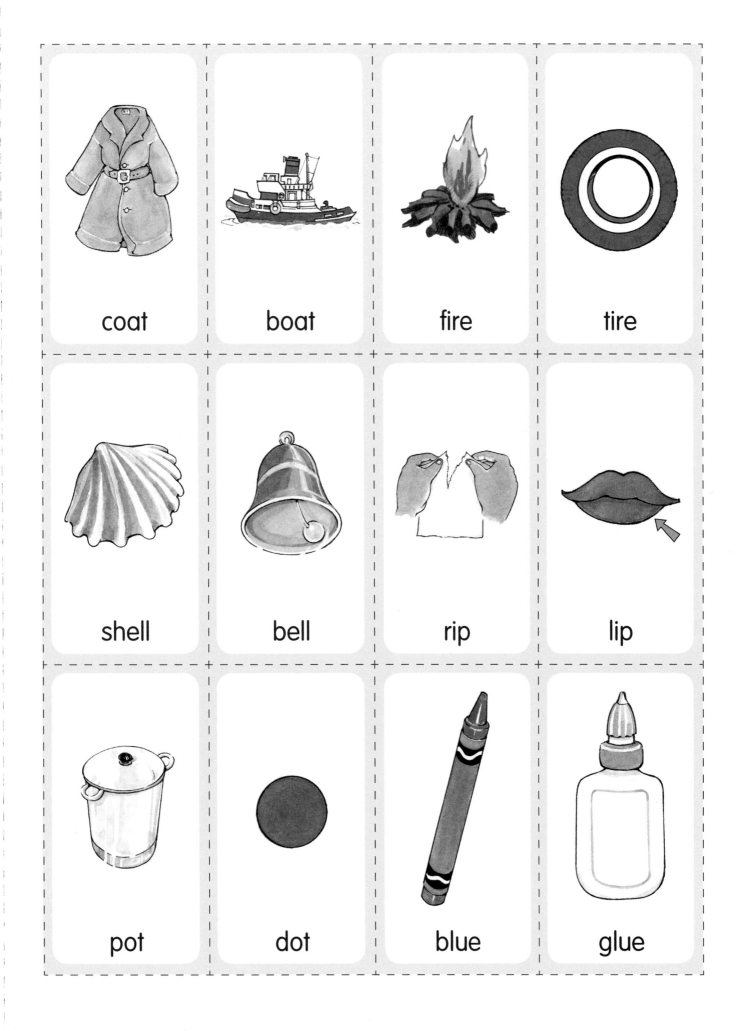

coat

boat

fire

tire

shell

bell

rip

lip

pot

dot

blue

glue

Game 3

Phonics Games, Level B
EMC 3363
© Evan-Moor Corp.

Game 3

Phonics Games, Level B
EMC 3363
© Evan-Moor Corp.

Game 3

Phonics Games, Level B
EMC 3363
© Evan-Moor Corp.

Game 3

Phonics Games, Level B
EMC 3363
© Evan-Moor Corp.

Game 3

Phonics Games, Level B
EMC 3363
© Evan-Moor Corp.

Game 3

Phonics Games, Level B
EMC 3363
© Evan-Moor Corp.

Game 3

Phonics Games, Level B
EMC 3363
© Evan-Moor Corp.

Game 3

Phonics Games, Level B
EMC 3363
© Evan-Moor Corp.

Game 3

Phonics Games, Level B
EMC 3363
© Evan-Moor Corp.

Game 3

Phonics Games, Level B
EMC 3363
© Evan-Moor Corp.

Game 3

Phonics Games, Level B
EMC 3363
© Evan-Moor Corp.

Game 3

Phonics Games, Level B
EMC 3363
© Evan-Moor Corp.

nose

hose

ring

king

sun

bun

cake

rake

pig

wig

nap

map

Game 3

Phonics Games, Level B
EMC 3363
© Evan-Moor Corp.

Game 3

Phonics Games, Level B
EMC 3363
© Evan-Moor Corp.

Game 3

Phonics Games, Level B
EMC 3363
© Evan-Moor Corp.

Game 3

Phonics Games, Level B
EMC 3363
© Evan-Moor Corp.

Game 3

Phonics Games, Level B
EMC 3363
© Evan-Moor Corp.

Game 3

Phonics Games, Level B
EMC 3363
© Evan-Moor Corp.

Game 3

Phonics Games, Level B
EMC 3363
© Evan-Moor Corp.

Game 3

Phonics Games, Level B
EMC 3363
© Evan-Moor Corp.

Game 3

Phonics Games, Level B
EMC 3363
© Evan-Moor Corp.

Game 3

Phonics Games, Level B
EMC 3363
© Evan-Moor Corp.

Game 3

Phonics Games, Level B
EMC 3363
© Evan-Moor Corp.

Game 3

Phonics Games, Level B
EMC 3363
© Evan-Moor Corp.

Answer Key

Matching rhyming words

How to Check:

1. Look at one of your pairs. Find the pictures on the answer key.

2. See if the pictures are next to each other on the answer key. If they are, you made a match.

3. Check your other pairs.

Color the Rhymes

Say each picture name.
Color the two pictures in each row that rhyme.

1.

2.

3.

4.

5.

6.

Name _____

I Spy

Read the words in the box. Use the words to complete the rhyme.

> eye   tree   pail   fog   rug   sky   log   hat

1. I spy with my little __eye_____

2. a on a _____,

3. a in a _____,

4. a by a _____,

5. a in the _____,

6. a in the _____,

7. a in a _____,

8. and a on a _____!

   Phonics Games, Level B • EMC 3363 • © Evan-Moor Corp.

Concentration

*Identifying short
vowel sounds*

Play

1. Place the orange picture cards and blue vowel cards facedown in rows.

2. Each player turns over one orange picture card and one blue vowel card and says the picture name aloud. If the picture name has the same vowel sound as the vowel, the player has a pair.

3. If the cards are a pair, the player keeps them. Then the player takes another turn and tries to make another pair.

4. If the cards are <u>not</u> a pair, the player turns them facedown. The next player picks two cards.

Win

1. Play continues until there are no more cards in the rows.

2. Players look at the answer key to see if their pairs are correctly matched.

3. The player with the most pairs wins!

Players need:

- 25 orange picture cards
- 25 blue vowel cards
- Answer key

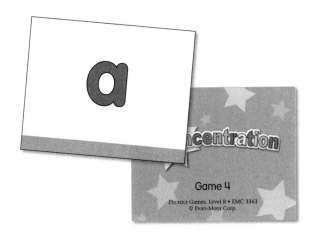

Phonics Games, Level B • EMC 3363 • © Evan-Moor Corp.

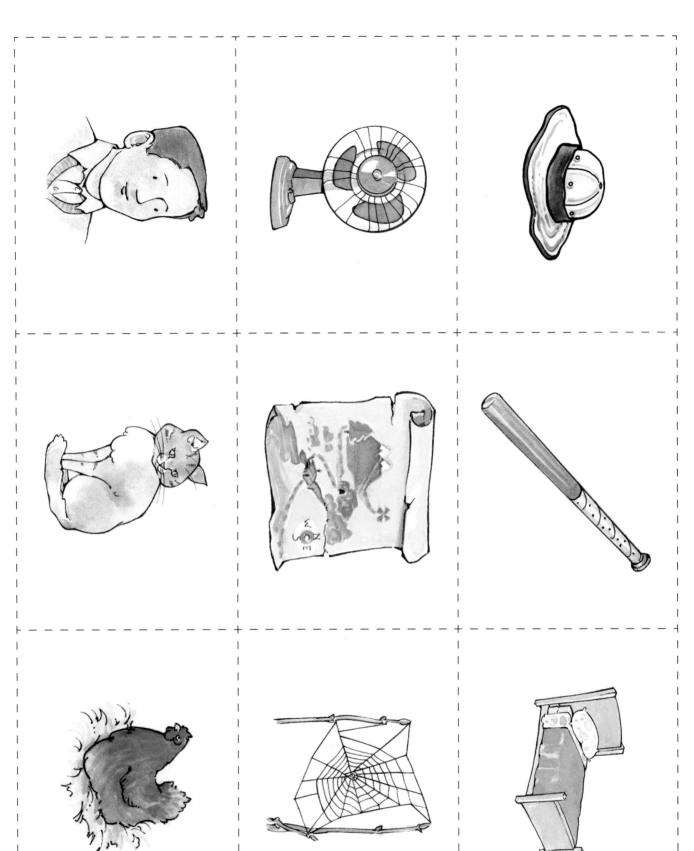

Concentration

Game 4

Concentration

Game 4

Concentration

Game 4

Concentration

Game 4

Concentration

Game 4

Concentration

Game 4

Concentration

Game 4

Concentration

Game 4

Concentration

Game 4

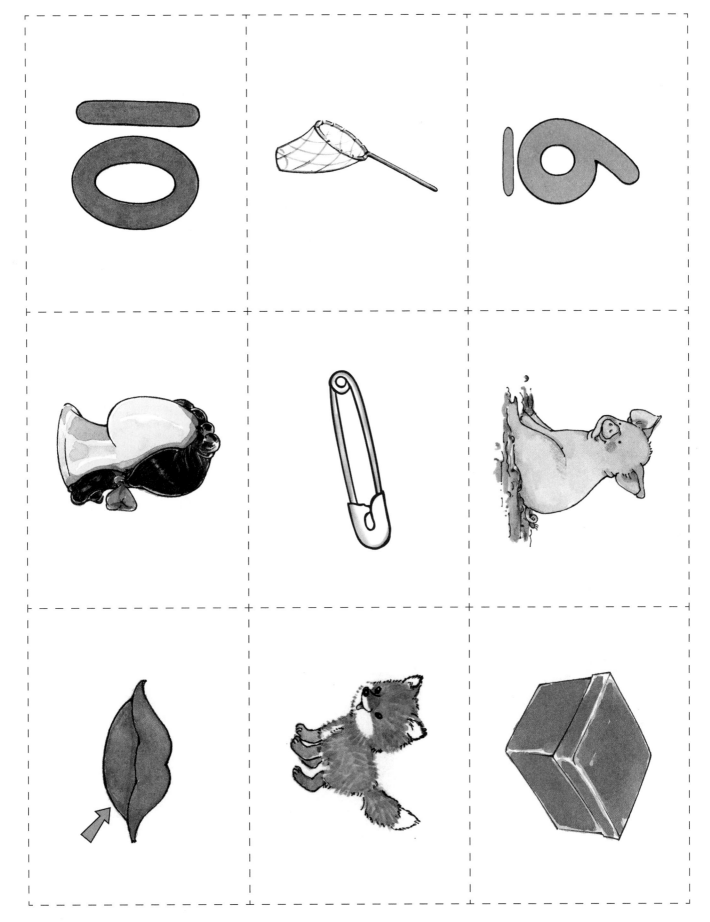

Concentration

Game 4

Phonics Games, Level B • EMC 3363
© Evan-Moor Corp.

Concentration

Game 4

Phonics Games, Level B • EMC 3363
© Evan-Moor Corp.

Concentration

Game 4

Phonics Games, Level B • EMC 3363
© Evan-Moor Corp.

Concentration

Game 4

Phonics Games, Level B • EMC 3363
© Evan-Moor Corp.

Concentration

Game 4

Phonics Games, Level B • EMC 3363
© Evan-Moor Corp.

Concentration

Game 4

Phonics Games, Level B • EMC 3363
© Evan-Moor Corp.

Concentration

Game 4

Phonics Games, Level B • EMC 3363
© Evan-Moor Corp.

Concentration

Game 4

Phonics Games, Level B • EMC 3363
© Evan-Moor Corp.

Concentration

Game 4

Phonics Games, Level B • EMC 3363
© Evan-Moor Corp.

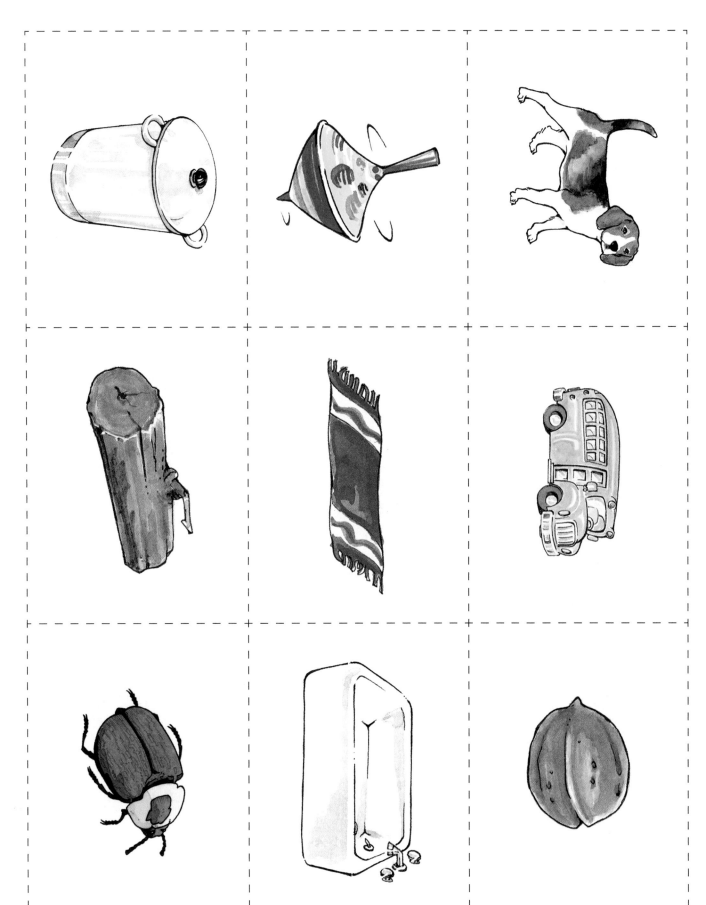

Game 4

Concentration

Phonics Games, Level B • EMC 3363
© Evan-Moor Corp.

Game 4

Concentration

Phonics Games, Level B • EMC 3363
© Evan-Moor Corp.

Game 4

Concentration

Phonics Games, Level B • EMC 3363
© Evan-Moor Corp.

Concentration

Game 4

Phonics Games, Level B • EMC 3363
© Evan-Moor Corp.

Concentration

Game 4

Phonics Games, Level B • EMC 3363
© Evan-Moor Corp.

Concentration

Game 4

Phonics Games, Level B • EMC 3363
© Evan-Moor Corp.

Concentration

Game 4

Phonics Games, Level B • EMC 3363
© Evan-Moor Corp.

Concentration

Game 4

Phonics Games, Level B • EMC 3363
© Evan-Moor Corp.

Concentration

Game 4

Phonics Games, Level B • EMC 3363
© Evan-Moor Corp.

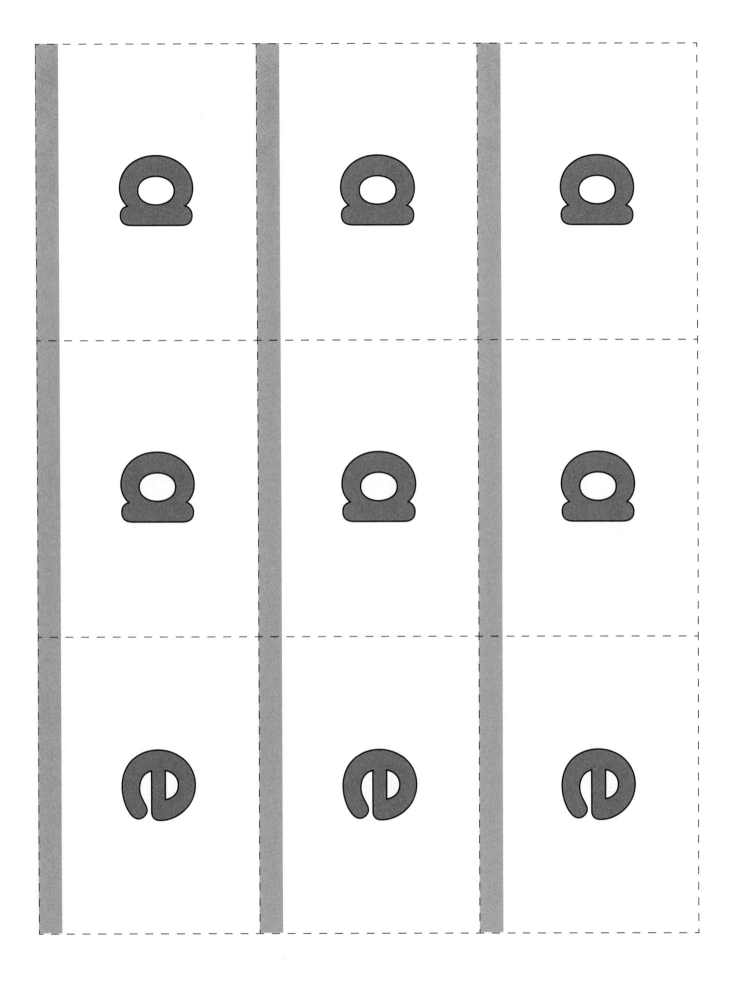

Concentration

Game 4

Phonics Games, Level B • EMC 3363
© Evan-Moor Corp.

Concentration

Game 4

Phonics Games, Level B • EMC 3363
© Evan-Moor Corp.

Concentration

Game 4

Phonics Games, Level B • EMC 3363
© Evan-Moor Corp.

Concentration

Game 4

Phonics Games, Level B • EMC 3363
© Evan-Moor Corp.

Concentration

Game 4

Phonics Games, Level B • EMC 3363
© Evan-Moor Corp.

Concentration

Game 4

Phonics Games, Level B • EMC 3363
© Evan-Moor Corp.

Concentration

Game 4

Phonics Games, Level B • EMC 3363
© Evan-Moor Corp.

Concentration

Game 4

Phonics Games, Level B • EMC 3363
© Evan-Moor Corp.

Concentration

Game 4

Phonics Games, Level B • EMC 3363
© Evan-Moor Corp.

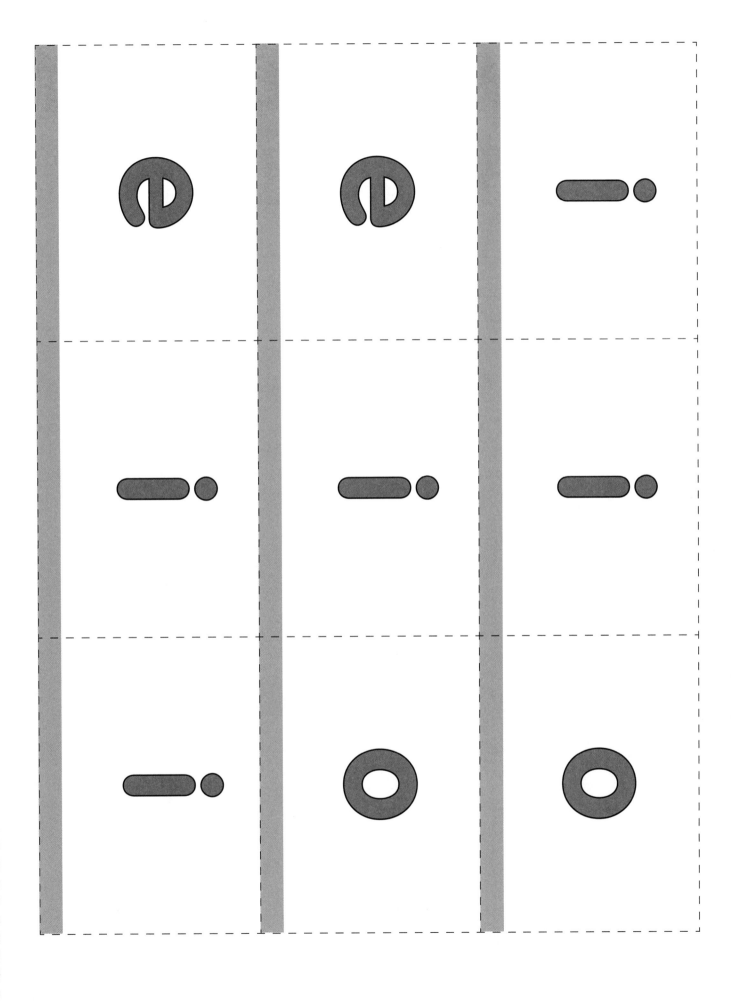

Concentration

Game 4

Concentration

Game 4

Concentration

Game 4

Concentration

Game 4

Concentration

Game 4

Concentration

Game 4

Concentration

Game 4

Concentration

Game 4

Concentration

Game 4

O O O

O ح ح

ح ح ح

Concentration

Game 4

Phonics Games, Level B • EMC 3363
© Evan-Moor Corp.

Concentration

Game 4

Phonics Games, Level B • EMC 3363
© Evan-Moor Corp.

Concentration

Game 4

Phonics Games, Level B • EMC 3363
© Evan-Moor Corp.

Concentration

Game 4

Phonics Games, Level B • EMC 3363
© Evan-Moor Corp.

Concentration

Game 4

Phonics Games, Level B • EMC 3363
© Evan-Moor Corp.

Concentration

Game 4

Phonics Games, Level B • EMC 3363
© Evan-Moor Corp.

Concentration

Game 4

Phonics Games, Level B • EMC 3363
© Evan-Moor Corp.

Concentration

Game 4

Phonics Games, Level B • EMC 3363
© Evan-Moor Corp.

Concentration

Game 4

Phonics Games, Level B • EMC 3363
© Evan-Moor Corp.

Concentration

Identifying short
vowel sounds

How to Check:

1. Look at one of your picture
   and vowel pairs. Find the
   vowel on the answer key.

2. Any of the pictures under that
   vowel make a correct pair.

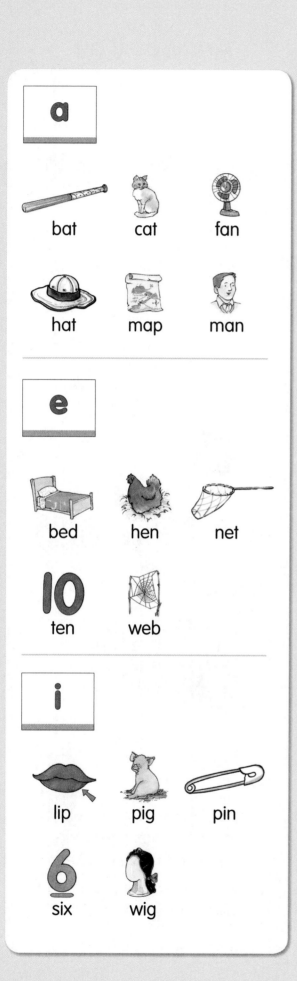

a

bat   cat   fan

hat   map   man

e

bed   hen   net

10
ten   web

i

lip   pig   pin

6
six   wig

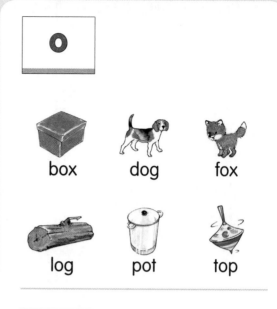

o

box   dog   fox

log   pot   top

u

bug   bus   nut

rug   tub

fold

Same Vowel Sounds

Say the first word in each row.
Put an ✗ on the picture whose name has the same vowel sound.

What's Missing?

Say the name of each picture. Listen for the short vowel sound.
Write the letter **a**, **e**, **i**, **o**, or **u** to complete the word.

1.	2.	3.
c _____ t	p _____ n	d _____ g
4.	5.	6.
l _____ g	b _____ g	w _____ b
7.	8.	9.
h _____ t	p _____ g	b _____ d

Phonics Games, Level B • EMC 3363 • © Evan-Moor Corp.

 in-a-row

Reading CVC words

Play

1. Distribute the boards and markers.
2. Put the picture cards into a bag.
3. The caller picks a picture card, shows the picture to the players, says the picture's name, and places it on the caller's board.
4. Players with the matching word on their boards place a marker on the word.
5. The caller picks a new card and play continues.

Win

1. A player must cover four words in a row to win. The words can go up and down, across, or diagonally.
2. The player calls out, "I win!"
3. Then the player reads aloud each word in the row as the caller checks the caller's board.
4. If the player's board and the caller's board match, then the player wins!

Each player needs:
- 1 game board
- Markers (such as beans)

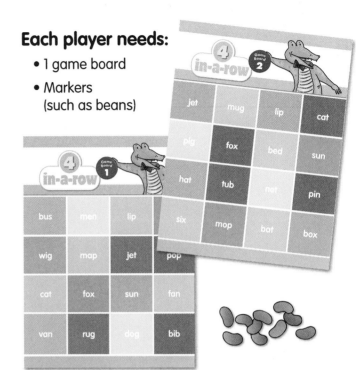

The caller needs:
- Caller's board
- 26 picture cards

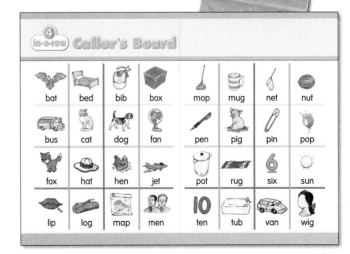

4 in-a-row

Game Board 1

bus	men	lip	ten
wig	map	jet	pop
cat	fox	sun	fan
van	rug	dog	bib

Game 5

Phonics Games, Level B
EMC 3363 • © Evan-Moor Corp.

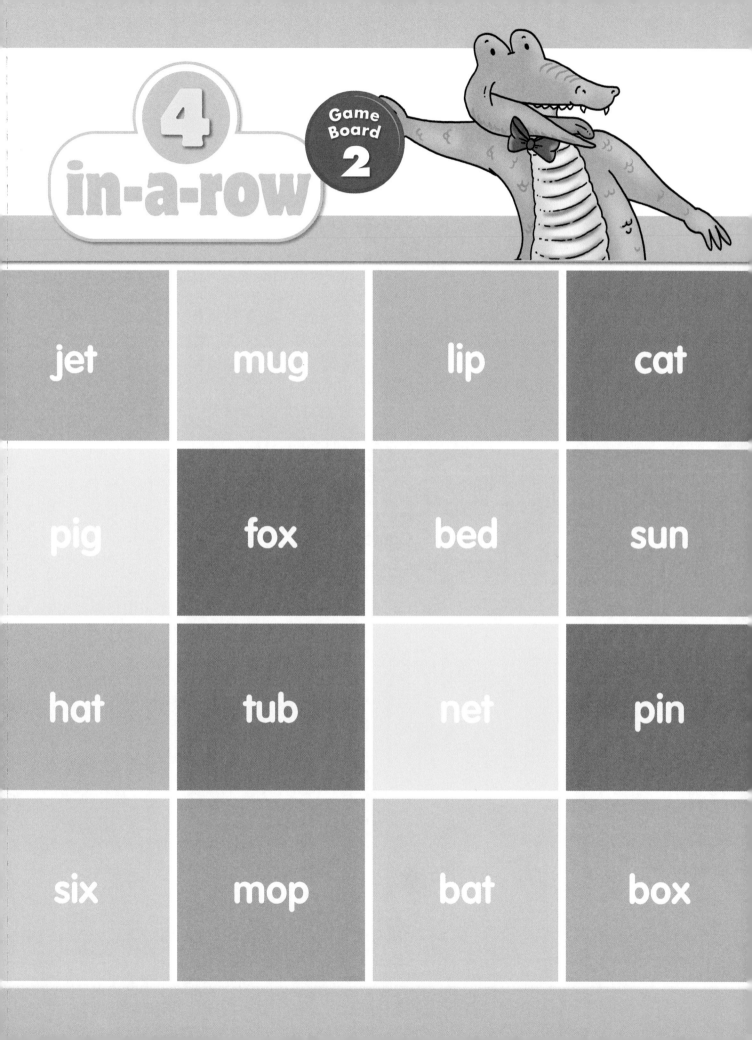

4 in-a-row

Game Board 2

jet	mug	lip	cat
pig	fox	bed	sun
hat	tub	net	pin
six	mop	bat	box

Game 5

Phonics Games, Level B
EMC 3363 • © Evan-Moor Corp.

box	wig	tub	hat
bed	sun	box	pot
van	lip	pig	men
fox	log	hen	mop

Game 5

Phonics Games, Level B
EMC 3363 • © Evan-Moor Corp.

4 in-a-row

Game Board 4

rug	hat	jet	pot
pen	box	cat	bib
mug	net	six	fox
ten	fan	wig	bus

Game 5

Phonics Games, Level B
EMC 3363 • © Evan-Moor Corp.

4 in-a-row

Game Board 5

ten	pin	cat	log
six	rug	pot	van
wig	bed	dog	sun
jet	mop	lip	fan

Game 5

Phonics Games, Level B
EMC 3363 • © Evan-Moor Corp.

4 in-a-row

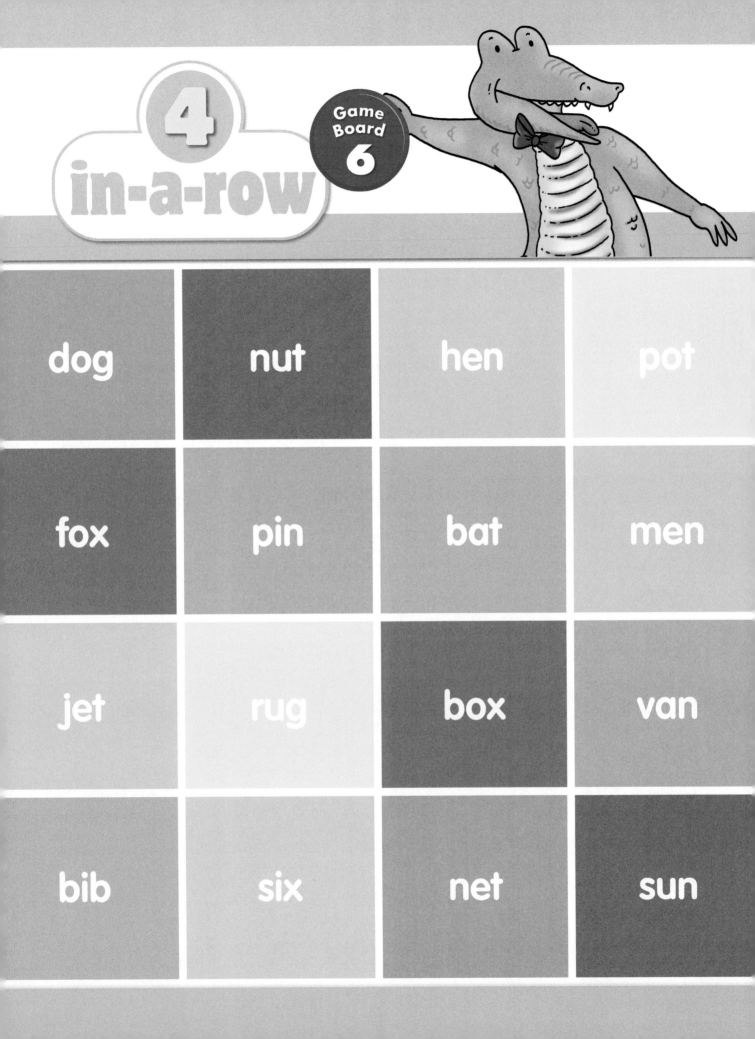

dog	nut	hen	pot
fox	pin	bat	men
jet	rug	box	van
bib	six	net	sun

Game 5

Phonics Games, Level B
EMC 3363 • © Evan-Moor Corp.

Game 5 • Picture Cards

Phonics Games, Level B
EMC 3363
© Evan-Moor Corp.

Game 5 • Picture Cards

Phonics Games, Level B
EMC 3363
© Evan-Moor Corp.

Game 5 • Picture Cards

Phonics Games, Level B
EMC 3363
© Evan-Moor Corp.

Game 5 • Picture Cards

Phonics Games, Level B
EMC 3363
© Evan-Moor Corp.

Game 5 • Picture Cards

Phonics Games, Level B
EMC 3363
© Evan-Moor Corp.

Game 5 • Picture Cards

Phonics Games, Level B
EMC 3363
© Evan-Moor Corp.

Game 5 • Picture Cards

Phonics Games, Level B
EMC 3363
© Evan-Moor Corp.

Game 5 • Picture Cards

Phonics Games, Level B
EMC 3363
© Evan-Moor Corp.

Game 5 • Picture Cards

Phonics Games, Level B
EMC 3363
© Evan-Moor Corp.

Game 5 • Picture Cards

Phonics Games, Level B
EMC 3363
© Evan-Moor Corp.

Game 5 • Picture Cards

Phonics Games, Level B
EMC 3363
© Evan-Moor Corp.

Game 5 • Picture Cards

Phonics Games, Level B
EMC 3363
© Evan-Moor Corp.

Game 5 • Picture Cards

Phonics Games, Level B
EMC 3363
© Evan-Moor Corp.

Game 5 • Picture Cards

Phonics Games, Level B
EMC 3363
© Evan-Moor Corp.

Game 5 • Picture Cards

Phonics Games, Level B
EMC 3363
© Evan-Moor Corp.

Game 5 • Picture Cards

Phonics Games, Level B
EMC 3363
© Evan-Moor Corp.

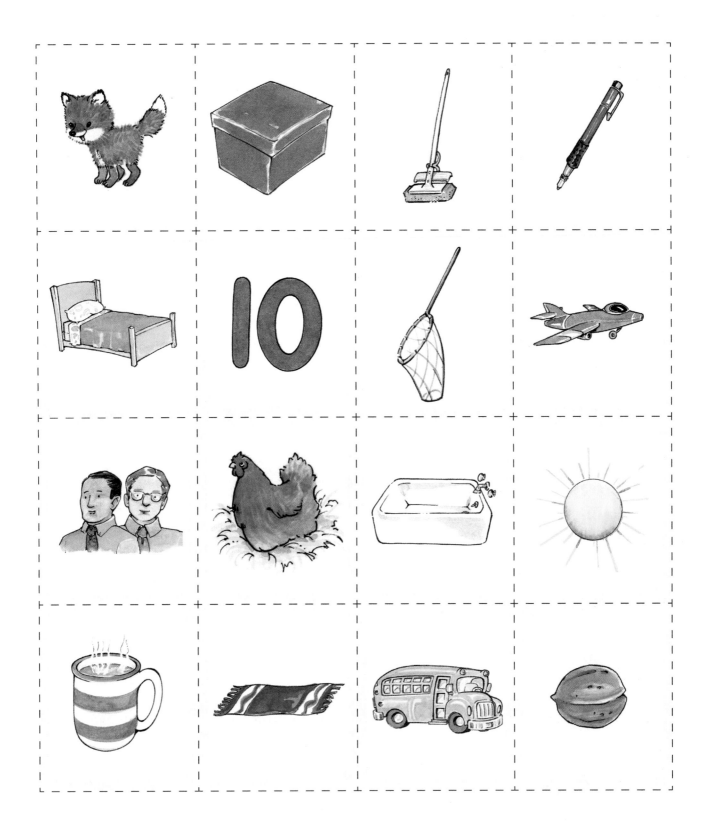

Game 5 • Picture Cards

Phonics Games, Level B
EMC 3363
© Evan-Moor Corp.

Game 5 • Picture Cards

Phonics Games, Level B
EMC 3363
© Evan-Moor Corp.

Game 5 • Picture Cards

Phonics Games, Level B
EMC 3363
© Evan-Moor Corp.

Game 5 • Picture Cards

Phonics Games, Level B
EMC 3363
© Evan-Moor Corp.

Game 5 • Picture Cards

Phonics Games, Level B
EMC 3363
© Evan-Moor Corp.

Game 5 • Picture Cards

Phonics Games, Level B
EMC 3363
© Evan-Moor Corp.

Game 5 • Picture Cards

Phonics Games, Level B
EMC 3363
© Evan-Moor Corp.

Game 5 • Picture Cards

Phonics Games, Level B
EMC 3363
© Evan-Moor Corp.

Game 5 • Picture Cards

Phonics Games, Level B
EMC 3363
© Evan-Moor Corp.

Game 5 • Picture Cards

Phonics Games, Level B
EMC 3363
© Evan-Moor Corp.

Game 5 • Picture Cards

Phonics Games, Level B
EMC 3363
© Evan-Moor Corp.

Game 5 • Picture Cards

Phonics Games, Level B
EMC 3363
© Evan-Moor Corp.

Game 5 • Picture Cards

Phonics Games, Level B
EMC 3363
© Evan-Moor Corp.

Game 5 • Picture Cards

Phonics Games, Level B
EMC 3363
© Evan-Moor Corp.

Game 5 • Picture Cards

Phonics Games, Level B
EMC 3363
© Evan-Moor Corp.

Game 5 • Picture Cards

Phonics Games, Level B
EMC 3363
© Evan-Moor Corp.

Game 5 • Caller's Board

Phonics Games, Level B
EMC 3363 • © Evan-Moor Corp.

bat

bed

bib

box

bus

cat

dog

fan

fox

hat

hen

jet

lip

log

map

men

mop	mug	net	nut
pen	pig	pin	pop
pot	rug	six	sun
ten	tub	van	wig

Game 5 • Caller's Board

Phonics Games, Level B
EMC 3363 • © Evan-Moor Corp.

What Do They Need?

Read each of the incomplete sentences and word choices.
Circle the word that best completes each sentence.

1. A  needs a _____.   bib   lid   bug

2. A needs a _____.   lap   log   hog

3. A ⚾ needs a _____.   bet   bat   mat

4. A 🐱 needs a _____.   mug   nut   rug

5. A 🎀 needs a _____.   fox   box   top

6. An needs a _____.   hen   ten   ham

Name _____

Read and Draw

Read each word.
Draw a picture that shows what each word means.

1. **bed**

2. **jet**

3. **sun**

4. **hat**

5. **wig**

6. **pot**

PING PANG POW!

Matching word family words

Play

1. Assign 3 players to each set. The first player picks a word family card from bag 1, says the word aloud, places the card in box 1 on the board, and says, "Ping."

2. The next player picks a word family card from bag 2 and says the word aloud. If the word is in the same word family as the word in box 1, the player says, "Pang" and places the card in box 2. Then the player goes to step 4.

3. If the word is <u>not</u> in the same word family, the player puts the card back into bag 2 and the next player draws a card. Play continues until a match is made.

4. The player who makes the match in box 2 draws from bag 3 and says the word aloud. If the word is in the same word family as boxes 1 and 2, the player puts the card in box 3 and says, "Pow! I win!"

5. If the word is <u>not</u> in the same word family, the player puts the card back and play continues until a player draws the winning card.

6. The winning player checks the answer key to make sure the words are part of the same word family. If they are, the player keeps all 3 cards and a new game begins.

Set **A** players need:

- Game board
- 21 cards
- Answer key
- 3 brown paper bags

Set **B** players need:

- Game board
- 21 cards
- Answer key
- 3 brown paper bags

Phonics Games, Level B • EMC 3363 • © Evan-Moor Corp.

POW!

3

PANG

2

PING

1

Game 6

Phonics Games, Level B
EMC 3363 • © Evan-Moor Corp.

POW!

3

PANG

2

PING

1

Game 6

Phonics Games, Level B
EMC 3363 • © Evan-Moor Corp.

jam

dad

did

bed

gum

not

dip

ham

bad

Game 6 • Set A

Phonics Games, Level B
EMC 3363 • © Evan-Moor Corp.

Game 6 • Set A

Phonics Games, Level B
EMC 3363 • © Evan-Moor Corp.

Game 6 • Set A

Phonics Games, Level B
EMC 3363 • © Evan-Moor Corp.

Game 6 • Set A

Phonics Games, Level B
EMC 3363 • © Evan-Moor Corp.

Game 6 • Set A

Phonics Games, Level B
EMC 3363 • © Evan-Moor Corp.

Game 6 • Set A

Phonics Games, Level B
EMC 3363 • © Evan-Moor Corp.

Game 6 • Set A

Phonics Games, Level B
EMC 3363 • © Evan-Moor Corp.

Game 6 • Set A

Phonics Games, Level B
EMC 3363 • © Evan-Moor Corp.

Game 6 • Set A

Phonics Games, Level B
EMC 3363 • © Evan-Moor Corp.

lid

fed

hum

hot

rip

Sam

sad

kid

red

Game 6 • Set A

Phonics Games, Level B
EMC 3363 • © Evan-Moor Corp.

Game 6 • Set A

Phonics Games, Level B
EMC 3363 • © Evan-Moor Corp.

Game 6 • Set A

Phonics Games, Level B
EMC 3363 • © Evan-Moor Corp.

Game 6 • Set A

Phonics Games, Level B
EMC 3363 • © Evan-Moor Corp.

Game 6 • Set A

Phonics Games, Level B
EMC 3363 • © Evan-Moor Corp.

Game 6 • Set A

Phonics Games, Level B
EMC 3363 • © Evan-Moor Corp.

Game 6 • Set A

Phonics Games, Level B
EMC 3363 • © Evan-Moor Corp.

Game 6 • Set A

Phonics Games, Level B
EMC 3363 • © Evan-Moor Corp.

Game 6 • Set A

Phonics Games, Level B
EMC 3363 • © Evan-Moor Corp.

yum   pot   sip

can   cap   pin

hop   bun   bat

Game 6 • Set A

Phonics Games, Level B
EMC 3363 • © Evan-Moor Corp.

Game 6 • Set A

Phonics Games, Level B
EMC 3363 • © Evan-Moor Corp.

Game 6 • Set A

Phonics Games, Level B
EMC 3363 • © Evan-Moor Corp.

Game 6 • Set B

Phonics Games, Level B
EMC 3363 • © Evan-Moor Corp.

Game 6 • Set B

Phonics Games, Level B
EMC 3363 • © Evan-Moor Corp.

Game 6 • Set B

Phonics Games, Level B
EMC 3363 • © Evan-Moor Corp.

Game 6 • Set B

Phonics Games, Level B
EMC 3363 • © Evan-Moor Corp.

Game 6 • Set B

Phonics Games, Level B
EMC 3363 • © Evan-Moor Corp.

Game 6 • Set B

Phonics Games, Level B
EMC 3363 • © Evan-Moor Corp.

get	man	map
win	mop	fun
hat	jet	pan

Game 6 • Set B

Phonics Games, Level B
EMC 3363 • © Evan-Moor Corp.

Game 6 • Set B

Phonics Games, Level B
EMC 3363 • © Evan-Moor Corp.

Game 6 • Set B

Phonics Games, Level B
EMC 3363 • © Evan-Moor Corp.

Game 6 • Set B

Phonics Games, Level B
EMC 3363 • © Evan-Moor Corp.

Game 6 • Set B

Phonics Games, Level B
EMC 3363 • © Evan-Moor Corp.

Game 6 • Set B

Phonics Games, Level B
EMC 3363 • © Evan-Moor Corp.

Game 6 • Set B

Phonics Games, Level B
EMC 3363 • © Evan-Moor Corp.

Game 6 • Set B

Phonics Games, Level B
EMC 3363 • © Evan-Moor Corp.

Game 6 • Set B

Phonics Games, Level B
EMC 3363 • © Evan-Moor Corp.

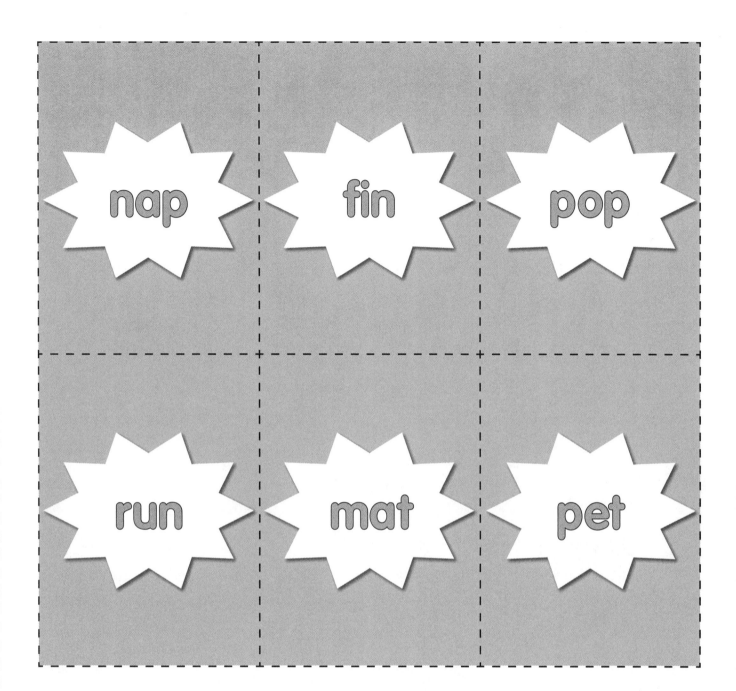

Game 6 • Set B

Phonics Games, Level B
EMC 3363 • © Evan-Moor Corp.

Game 6 • Set B

Phonics Games, Level B
EMC 3363 • © Evan-Moor Corp.

Game 6 • Set B

Phonics Games, Level B
EMC 3363 • © Evan-Moor Corp.

Game 6 • Set B

Phonics Games, Level B
EMC 3363 • © Evan-Moor Corp.

Game 6 • Set B

Phonics Games, Level B
EMC 3363 • © Evan-Moor Corp.

Game 6 • Set B

Phonics Games, Level B
EMC 3363 • © Evan-Moor Corp.

Set A

Answer Key

Matching word family words

How to Check:

1. Look at your set of three cards. Find one of the words on the answer key.

2. Look at the words next to it. Do they match your set?

3. If they do, you win!

Set B

Answer Key

Matching word family words

How to Check:

1. Look at your set of three cards. Find one of the words on the answer key.

2. Look at the words next to it. Do they match your set?

3. If they do, you win!

1. can   man   pan

2. cap   map   nap

3. pin   win   fin

4. hop   mop   pop

5. bun   fun   run

6. bat   hat   mat

7. get   jet   pet

1. jam   ham   Sam

2. dad   bad   sad

3. did   lid   kid

4. bed   fed   red

5. gum   hum   yum

6. not   hot   pot

7. dip   rip   sip

Name _____

Word Family Worms

Cut out each word at the bottom of the page.
Glue each word onto the matching word family worm.

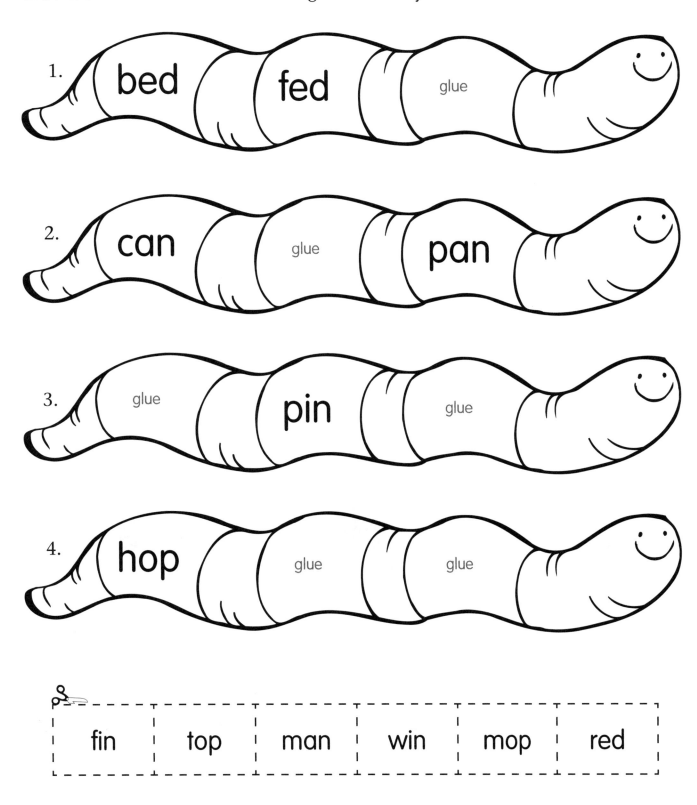

1. bed   fed   glue

2. can   glue   pan

3. glue   pin   glue

4. hop   glue   glue

✂

| fin | top | man | win | mop | red |

Name _____

Families of Words

Circle the word that names each picture.
Then write a new word for each word family.

1.

(bat) cat hat

sat
_____

2.

had mad dad

_____

3.

cot dot pot

_____

4.

hip zip rip

_____

5.

wet get net

_____

6.

rug bug pug

_____

Phonics Games, Level B • EMC 3363 • © Evan-Moor Corp.

Spell It!

Spelling CVC words

Each player needs:

• 1 game board

Play

1. Players look at the pictures on their game boards and think about which letters they need to spell each picture name.

2. The first player picks a letter out of the bag. If the player needs the letter to spell a word, he or she places the letter in the correct box on his or her game board and takes another turn.

3. If the player does <u>not</u> need the letter, he or she puts it back into the bag and the next player takes a turn.

Put the cards into a bag.

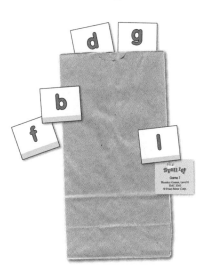

Answer key

Win

1. The first player to spell all three words shouts out, "Spell it!"

2. Players check the answer key to see if the words are spelled correctly.

3. If the player who shouted "Spell it!" spelled all three words correctly, he or she wins!

Spell It!

  a

  e

  i

Game 7

Phonics Games, Level B
EMC 3363 • © Evan-Moor Corp.

Spell It!

  i

  o

 u

Game 7

Phonics Games, Level B
EMC 3363 • © Evan-Moor Corp.

Spell It!

i

u

a

Game 7

Phonics Games, Level B
EMC 3363 • © Evan-Moor Corp.

Spell It!

 u

 a

 e

Spell It!

Game 7

Phonics Games, Level B
EMC 3363 • © Evan-Moor Corp.

Spell It!

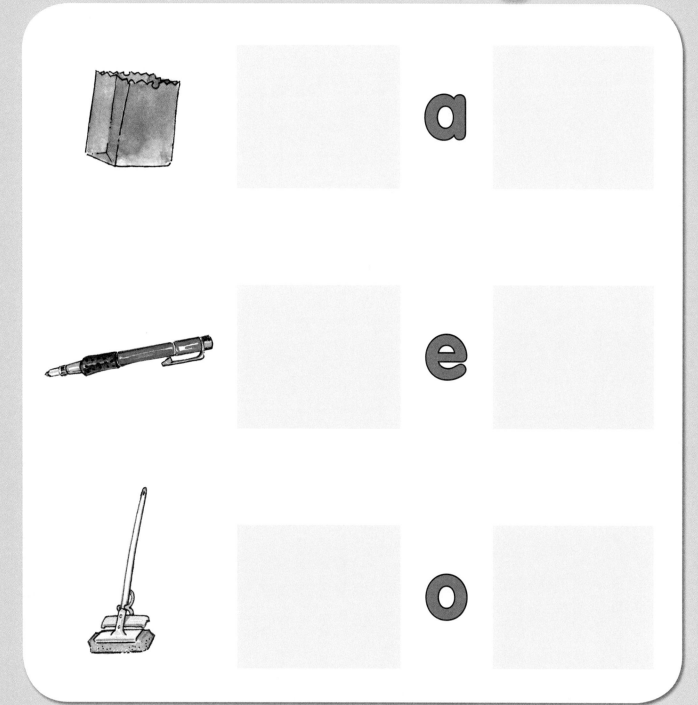

a

e

o

Game 7

Phonics Games, Level B
EMC 3363 • © Evan-Moor Corp.

Spell It!

e

6

i

o

Game 7

Phonics Games, Level B
EMC 3363 • © Evan-Moor Corp.

b	d	g	g
b	d	g	g
b	d	g	h
b	f	g	h
b	f	g	l
b	f	g	l

Spell It!

Game 7

Phonics Games, Level B
EMC 3363
© Evan-Moor Corp.

Spell It!

Game 7

Phonics Games, Level B
EMC 3363
© Evan-Moor Corp.

Spell It!

Game 7

Phonics Games, Level B
EMC 3363
© Evan-Moor Corp.

Spell It!

Game 7

Phonics Games, Level B
EMC 3363
© Evan-Moor Corp.

Spell It!

Game 7

Phonics Games, Level B
EMC 3363
© Evan-Moor Corp.

Spell It!

Game 7

Phonics Games, Level B
EMC 3363
© Evan-Moor Corp.

Spell It!

Game 7

Phonics Games, Level B
EMC 3363
© Evan-Moor Corp.

Spell It!

Game 7

Phonics Games, Level B
EMC 3363
© Evan-Moor Corp.

Spell It!

Game 7

Phonics Games, Level B
EMC 3363
© Evan-Moor Corp.

Spell It!

Game 7

Phonics Games, Level B
EMC 3363
© Evan-Moor Corp.

Spell It!

Game 7

Phonics Games, Level B
EMC 3363
© Evan-Moor Corp.

Spell It!

Game 7

Phonics Games, Level B
EMC 3363
© Evan-Moor Corp.

Spell It!

Game 7

Phonics Games, Level B
EMC 3363
© Evan-Moor Corp.

Spell It!

Game 7

Phonics Games, Level B
EMC 3363
© Evan-Moor Corp.

Spell It!

Game 7

Phonics Games, Level B
EMC 3363
© Evan-Moor Corp.

Spell It!

Game 7

Phonics Games, Level B
EMC 3363
© Evan-Moor Corp.

Spell It!

Game 7

Phonics Games, Level B
EMC 3363
© Evan-Moor Corp.

Spell It!

Game 7

Phonics Games, Level B
EMC 3363
© Evan-Moor Corp.

Spell It!

Game 7

Phonics Games, Level B
EMC 3363
© Evan-Moor Corp.

Spell It!

Game 7

Phonics Games, Level B
EMC 3363
© Evan-Moor Corp.

Spell It!

Game 7

Phonics Games, Level B
EMC 3363
© Evan-Moor Corp.

Spell It!

Game 7

Phonics Games, Level B
EMC 3363
© Evan-Moor Corp.

Spell It!

Game 7

Phonics Games, Level B
EMC 3363
© Evan-Moor Corp.

Spell It!

Game 7

Phonics Games, Level B
EMC 3363
© Evan-Moor Corp.

l	n	p	w
m	n	p	w
m	n	r	w
m	p	r	x
m	p	s	x
n	p	t	x

Spell It!

Game 7

Phonics Games, Level B
EMC 3363
© Evan-Moor Corp.

Spell It!

Game 7

Phonics Games, Level B
EMC 3363
© Evan-Moor Corp.

Spell It!

Game 7

Phonics Games, Level B
EMC 3363
© Evan-Moor Corp.

Spell It!

Game 7

Phonics Games, Level B
EMC 3363
© Evan-Moor Corp.

Spell It!

Game 7

Phonics Games, Level B
EMC 3363
© Evan-Moor Corp.

Spell It!

Game 7

Phonics Games, Level B
EMC 3363
© Evan-Moor Corp.

Spell It!

Game 7

Phonics Games, Level B
EMC 3363
© Evan-Moor Corp.

Spell It!

Game 7

Phonics Games, Level B
EMC 3363
© Evan-Moor Corp.

Spell It!

Game 7

Phonics Games, Level B
EMC 3363
© Evan-Moor Corp.

Spell It!

Game 7

Phonics Games, Level B
EMC 3363
© Evan-Moor Corp.

Spell It!

Game 7

Phonics Games, Level B
EMC 3363
© Evan-Moor Corp.

Spell It!

Game 7

Phonics Games, Level B
EMC 3363
© Evan-Moor Corp.

Spell It!

Game 7

Phonics Games, Level B
EMC 3363
© Evan-Moor Corp.

Spell It!

Game 7

Phonics Games, Level B
EMC 3363
© Evan-Moor Corp.

Spell It!

Game 7

Phonics Games, Level B
EMC 3363
© Evan-Moor Corp.

Spell It!

Game 7

Phonics Games, Level B
EMC 3363
© Evan-Moor Corp.

Spell It!

Game 7

Phonics Games, Level B
EMC 3363
© Evan-Moor Corp.

Spell It!

Game 7

Phonics Games, Level B
EMC 3363
© Evan-Moor Corp.

Spell It!

Game 7

Phonics Games, Level B
EMC 3363
© Evan-Moor Corp.

Spell It!

Game 7

Phonics Games, Level B
EMC 3363
© Evan-Moor Corp.

Spell It!

Game 7

Phonics Games, Level B
EMC 3363
© Evan-Moor Corp.

Spell It!

Game 7

Phonics Games, Level B
EMC 3363
© Evan-Moor Corp.

Spell It!

Game 7

Phonics Games, Level B
EMC 3363
© Evan-Moor Corp.

Spell It!

Game 7

Phonics Games, Level B
EMC 3363
© Evan-Moor Corp.

How to Check:

1. Find the picture that shows your game board.

2. Check to see if you spelled the words correctly.

Spell It! — 1

🦇	b	a	t
🛏️	b	e	d
👩	w	i	g

Spell It! — 2

🐷	p	i	g
🐕	d	o	g
☕	m	u	g

Spell It! — 3

👄	l	i	p
🧶	r	u	g
🗺️	m	a	p

Spell It! — 4

🐞	b	u	g
🪭	f	a	n
🐔	h	e	n

Spell It! — 5

📕	b	a	g
🖊️	p	e	n
🧹	m	o	p

Spell It! — 6

👨‍👨	m	e	n
6	s	i	x
🦊	f	o	x

fold

Name _____

Watch Me Spell!

Use the letters.
Write the word next to each picture.

1.  g m u _____

2.  t n e _____

3.  t a b _____

4.  a p m _____

5.  i p g _____

6.   a g b _____

Missing Letters

Write the missing letter to spell each word.

1.  ____eb	2.  fo____	3.  f____n
4.  ____ix	5.  b____s	6.  ca____
7.  m____n	8.  cu____	9.  ____ed

Phonics Games Answer Key

LEVEL
B

Page 25—Animal Sounds

1. m
2. p
3. b
4. r
5. l
6. h
7. d
8. t
9. w

Page 26—What's the Sound?

1. b
2. f
3. n
4. s
5. g
6. r

Page 43—How Does It End?

1. t
2. g
3. d
4. s
5. m
6. l
7. r
8. b
9. n

Page 44—End It

1. p
2. f
3. k
4. t
5. s
6. l
7. n
8. m

Page 57—Color the Rhymes

1. cake   rake
2. glue   two
3. bug   rug
4. three   tree
5. pig   wig
6. car   star

Page 58—I Spy

1. eye
2. log
3. rug
4. tree
5. sky
6. fog
7. hat
8. pail

Page 75—Same Vowel Sounds

1. hen
2. wig
3. map
4. top
5. bus
6. cat

Page 76—What's Missing?

1. a
2. i
3. o
4. o
5. u
6. e
7. a
8. i
9. e

Page 99—What Do They Need?

1. bib
2. log
3. bat
4. rug
5. box
6. hen

Page 100—Read and Draw

Pictures will vary.

Page 119—Word Family Worms

1. red
2. man
3. fin, win
4. top, mop

Page 120—Families of Words

1. bat
2. dad
3. pot
4. zip
5. wet
6. bug

Page 141—Watch Me Spell!

1. mug
2. net
3. bat
4. map
5. pig
6. bag

Page 142—Missing Letters

1. web
2. fox
3. fan
4. six
5. bus
6. can
7. men
8. cup
9. bed

Word Family Games:
Centers for Up to 6 Players
Level A • EMC 3357

Word Family Games:
Centers for Up to 6 Players

Word Family Games: Centers for Up to 6 Players provides fun, hands-on practice to increase word recognition and vocabulary skills. Each book contains 7 full-color games with materials for six players and a leader, plus two reproducible activity pages for extra word family practice. Word families practiced correspond to those presented in *Word Family Stories and Activities.* Students will eagerly practice word family words while trying to be the first to call "Bingo!" or "Four in a Row!" 144 full-color pages.
Correlated to state standards.

Word Family Games, Level A
Grades K–2   EMC 3357

Word Family Games, Level C
Grades 1–3   EMC 3359

Word Family Games, Level B
Grades K–2   EMC 3358

Word Family Games, Level D
Grades 1–3   EMC 3360

High-Frequency Words:
Center Games
Level A • EMC 3380

High-Frequency Words: Center Games

High-Frequency Words: Center Games contains colorful and engaging game formats that provide students with the motivation they need to practice reading high-frequency words. Each of the four books provides practice based on Dolch Basic Sight Vocabulary, as well as words from Fry's Instant Words lists. Games such as Bingo, Concentration, and Ping, Pang, Pow! make high-frequency word recognition practice fun! 144 full-color pages.
Correlated to state standards.

High-Frequency Words:
Center Games, Level A
Grades K–1   EMC 3380

High-Frequency Words:
Center Games, Level C
Grades 2–3   EMC 3382

High-Frequency Words:
Center Games, Level B
Grades K–1   EMC 3381

High-Frequency Words:
Center Games, Level D
Grades 2–3   EMC 3383